Quotes for Personal Excellence – 8

Work

One Hundred Quotes and Thoughts
with One Hundred Insightful Illustrations of Lord Ganesha

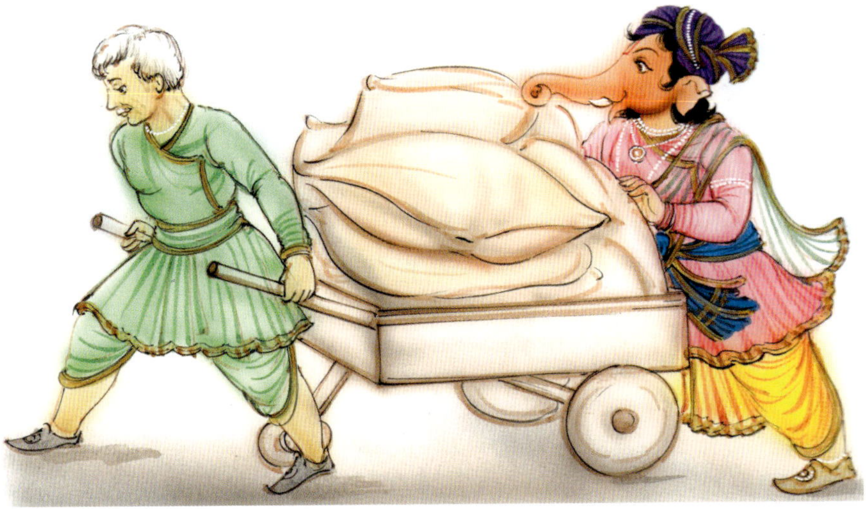

R.N. Kogata • Lalita Kogata

DK PRINTWORLD
Publishers of Indian Traditions

First Published in India, 2015
ISBN 13: 978-81-246-0760-2
ISBN 10: 81-246-0760-5

A creation of:
Mr R.N. Kogata and Mrs Lalita Kogata
608, Hiran Magari, Sector - 11, Udaipur, India
Phones: +91-94141 58870, +91-294-258 3870
devkush@rediffmail.com

Printed and published by:
D.K. Printworld (P) Ltd.
'Vedasri', F-395, Sudarshan Park
(Metro Station: Ramesh Nagar), New Delhi - 110 015
Phones: 011-2545 3975, 2546 6019 Fax: 011-2546 5926
e-mail: indology@dkprintworld.com Web: www.dkprintworld.com

Preface

"Work is worship". This is a very old proverb which means there is no better way to worship God than being hard-working. This is fully justified because what man has achieved during the course of his development is a result of hard work over a long period of time. He owes all his greatness to hard work. Hence, it is the root of all success.

There is no alternative to hard-work. Today man has conquered in some way nature, he has set foot on the moon, he has traveled in the space, he has invented so many life-saving drugs and all these became possible because he never neglected work. We see wonderful progress in the fields of agriculture and industry too. The methods of agriculture have been improved, resulting in the growth of production. Now the farmers are enjoying better days than what they had in the past. This is again the result of hard work. Indeed work is worship.

There is an old proverb, "God helps those who help themselves". God also gets impressed, helps and cooperates only with those who are hardworking and sincere. God does not love being worshipped by a person each second. He wants that a person should work hard. So, it is not praiseworthy if we worship God all the time and do not work at all.

There are people who believe that it is luck that plays super role in everybody's life. Hence, they avoid work and wait for the miracles, which according to them must occur in their life and consequently they would get all those things which they wish for. But in reality no such miracle happens particularly when we don't work.

By hard-working and with sincerity only, one can hope for miracles. So, we must think that God has made us with some purpose and for achieving that purpose He has sent us into the world — the world of work. Now, it is our humble duty to utilize each and every minute in the best possible way. We have to utilize our potentialities to the full so that we may be counted among the successful persons of the world.

Here, we should be alert that when we say that "work is worship" we mean work which is useful and wholesome for the society. Work, which is harmful for the society, can never be praiseworthy. Hence, our potentialities should be utilized in constructive works, not in making some poisonous drugs or destructive weapons or in planning some conspiracy or waging wars or in doing anti-social activities. These can never be a blessing for mankind nor can these make God happy. Our work must be creative and it must have some humble base. Only then we can say "work is worship", otherwise it will be devil's worship.

India has a rich heritage of hard-working people such as Mahatma Gandhi, Dr Rajendra Prasad, Jawahar Lal Nehru and Sardar Patel. We should learn from them and work for the benefit of the nation at large.

We also need to realize when do our efforts succeed and when do they not, and a required exertion is necessary for us to consider anything as work, we may enjoy it too, and also, feel some necessity to bring about the outcome. Our mind has registered a plan, a path our action will follow, and also, what we will look to avoid, and in recognizing the earliest indications of this negative effect lies a measure of our skill. Actually a large component of our skill lies in avoiding the unwanted from happening, which can perhaps happen in many ways.

It is important to consider the scope of our effort and know that there are other parts linked to it, and their movement is going to affect our efforts.

In the modern society, people need to work hard in order to achieve their goals. An individual, who possesses a higher level of working abilities, has a greater chance of success. The working abilities include skills to work independently or abilities to work with a group of people on a team. And may be the group effort and cooperation within are more likely to accomplish greater achievements compared to working alone.

In order to understand it more realistically, we have conceived the idea of this book to tell you much more about work in just few hours. These meaningful quotes about work will touch, inspire and move you, and you can thus more easily understand doing and completing the work successfully.

This book contains 100 carefully chosen quotations on Work, mixed, modified and created. Some of the thoughts presented are ours and others are from the people who have stood by and worked for the values; some were famous and some others were ordinary people. We have tried to indicate in the acknowledgment page the persons who have quoted wherever we could remember. Our sincere thanks to all these great personalities and eminent writers; who have given such invaluable thoughts to this world. Any amendment/addition in this regard is most welcome from the readers.

Ganesha gives peace, prosperity and wisdom. Therefore, each of the quotes in this book has a painting of Lord Ganesha to inspire you. These paintings have been created by our professional artists keeping in view themes of individual quotation.

We prostrate before our parents Smt Kanchan Devi and Shri Bhairav Lal Kogata, and late Kamla Devi Nuwal and late Prof. K.M. Nuwal, whose blessings have enabled us to grow in life.

Expecting blessings and constructive feedback from all of you,

Lalita and **R.N. Kogata**

Work

One Hundred Quotes and Thoughts
with One Hundred Insightful Illustrations of Lord Ganesha

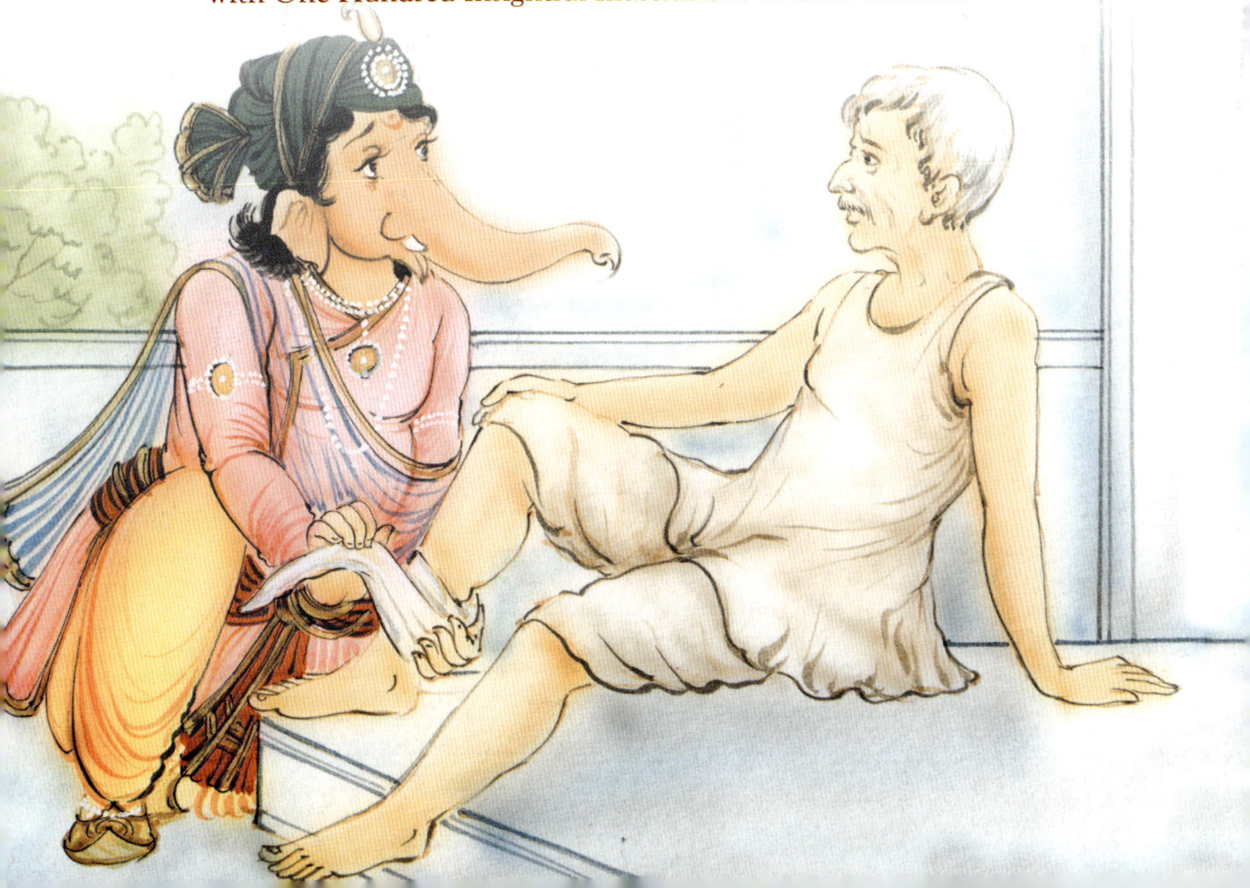

Acknowledgement

Quotations from some eminent writers, philosophers and great personalities have been included in this book. Details of the same are given below. We sincerely thank all of them.

Page No.	Quotation by	Page No.	Quotation by	Page No.	Quotation by	Page No.	Quotation by
W-1	John Lubbock	W-25	Margaret Mead	W-49	Walter Gropius	W-73	Pearl S. Buck
W-3	Calvin Coolidge	W-28	Ogden Nash	W-50	Jawaharlal Nehru	W-74	Sarah Bolton
W-4	Ella W. Wilcox	W-29	Sir Philip Sidney	W-51	Eric Hoffer	W-75	Robert Frostson
W-5	Lao-Tzu	W-30	John Ruskin	W-52	Howard Newton	W-76	Henry Ford
W-6	W. Kelly Griffith	W-31	John Ruskin	W-54	Frederick Douglass	W-79	Nancy Coey
W-7	Thomas A. Edi	W-32	Helene Lagerberg	W-55	Peter Drucker	W-80	William James
W-8	John Burroughs	W-33	Sam Ewing	W-56	Aristotle	W-82	Jean de la Bruyere
W-9	Martha L. Hoffman	W-34	Mahatma Gandhi	W-57	Henry Ford	W-83	Michael Bridge
W-10	Gary Sinise	W-35	Anne Frank	W-58	Mahatma Gandhi	W-84	Betty Bender
W-11	Roger Staubach	W-36	Jeanette Winterson	W-59	David Bly	W-85	Nancy Coey
W-13	Theodore Roosevelt	W-37	Sir William Osler	W-60	John R. Woolen	W-86	Eleanor Roosevelt
W-14	Franklin Roosevelt	W-38	Jawaharlal Nehru	W-61	Garson Kanin	W-87	Henry J. Kaiser
W-15	Steve Pavlina	W-39	Reese Witherspoon	W-62	William Osler	W-88	Walter Chrysler
W-17	Louisa May Alcott	W-40	Margaret Fuller	W-63	Georgia O'Keeffe	W-90	Albert Camus
W-18	Dr Thomas Fuller	W-41	Edwin H. Stuart	W-65	John Ruskin	W-91	Khalil Gibran
W-19	Donald Trump	W-42	Indira Gandhi	W-66	Elbert Hubbard	W-92	George Sand
W-20	Margaret Thatcher	W-43	Oprah Winfrey	W-67	Mark Twain	W-95	James Allen
W-21	Pearl S. Buck	W-44	Oliver Schreiner	W-68	Harry S. Truman	W-96	Voltaire
W-22	Walter Chrysler	W-45	David Sarnoff	W-69	Richard Bach	W-97	Merle Shain
W-23	Michael Jordan	W-46	Henry Ford	W-70	Donald Kendall	W-98	Randall Munroe
W-24	Louise Nevelson	W-47	Hannah More	W-71	Harry Golden	W-99	Charles W. Eliot

A day of worry
is more exhausting
than a day of work.

A successful man
continues to look for work
after he has found a job.

All growth depends upon activity.
There is no development
physically or intellectually
without effort,
and effort means work.

Always continue the climb.

It is possible for you
to do whatever you choose,
if you first get to know
who you are and
are willing to work with a power
that is greater than ourselves
to do it.

An ant on the move
does more than
a dozing ox.

Any necessary work
that pays an honest wage
carries its own honour and dignity.

Being busy does not
always mean real work.

The object of all work is
production or accomplishment,
and to either of these ends
there must be forethought,
system, planning, intelligence,
and honest purpose,
as well as perspiration.

Seeming to do is not doing.

Blessed is the man
who has some congenial work,
some occupation in which
he can put his heart,
that provides a complete outlet
to all the forces within him.

W-8

Call no work low that is honest.

Honest toil never degrades.

Careers, like rockets,
don't always take off on schedule.

The key is
to keep working the engines.

Confidence is
the result of
hours and days
and weeks and years
of constant work
and dedication.

Every day I get up
and look through the Forbes list
of the richest people in the world.

If I'm not there, I go to work
and do it with enjoyment.

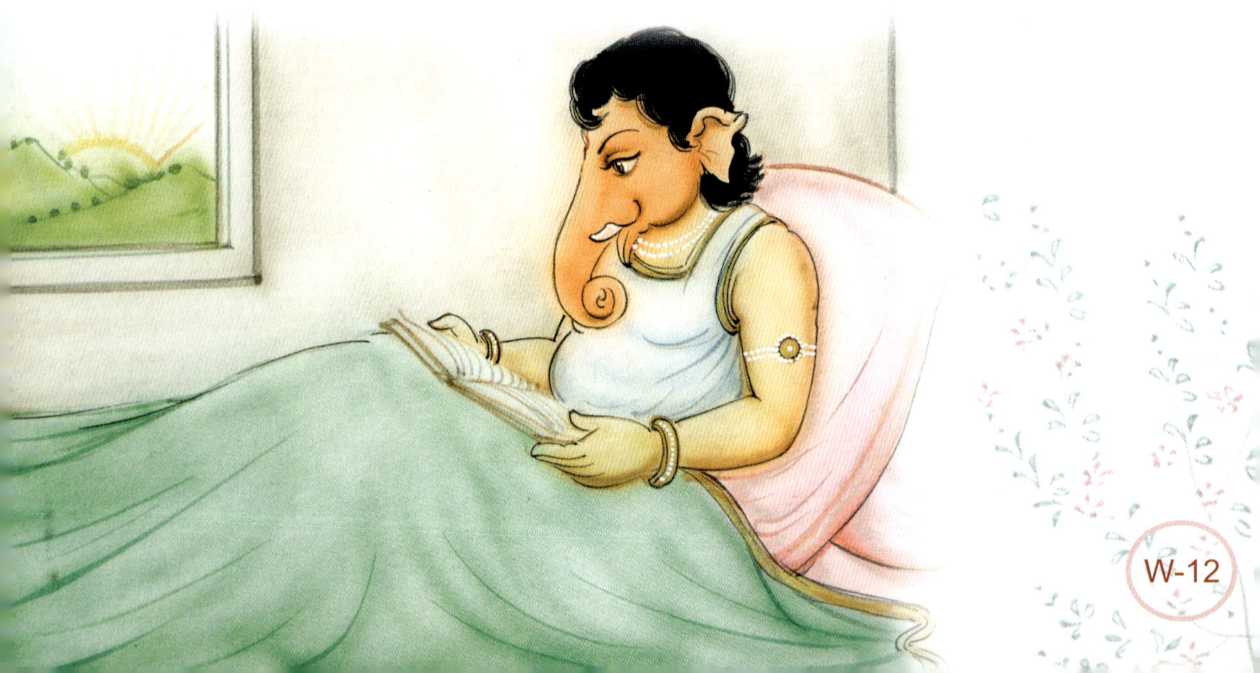

Far and away
the best prize that life offers
is the chance to work hard
at work worth doing.

Happiness is
not in the mere possession of money;

it lies in the joy of achievement,
in the thrill of work
and creative effort.

W-14

Hard work is painful
when life is devoid of purpose.

But when you live for
something greater than yourself
and the gratification of your own ego,
then hard work becomes a labour of love.

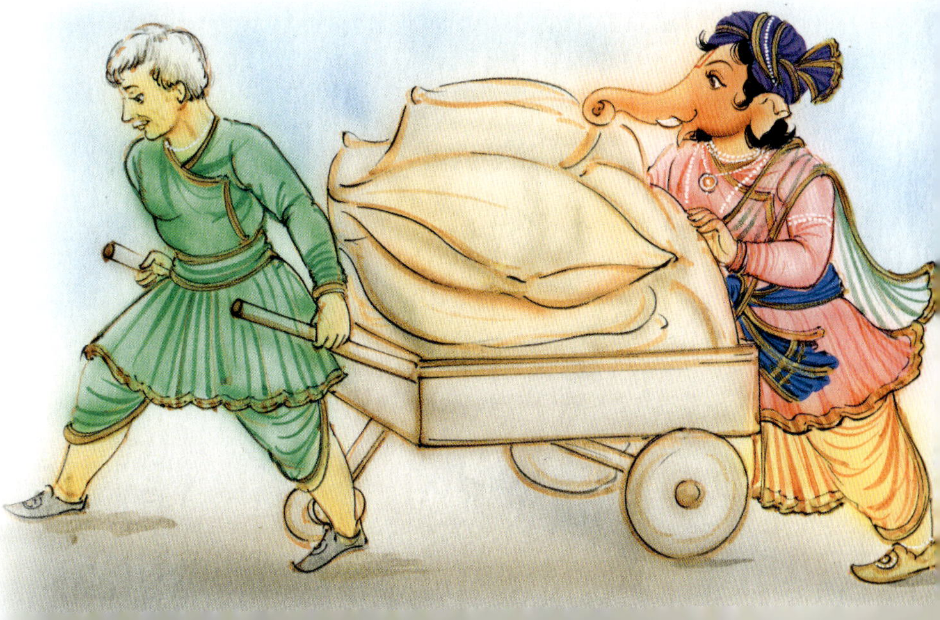

Hard work
may not guarantee success,
but improves its chances.

W-16

Have regular hours for work and play;
make each day useful and pleasant,
and prove that you understand the worth
of time by employing it well.

Then youth will be delightful,
old age will bring minimum regrets,
and life becomes a beautiful success,
in spite of poverty.

He who would have the fruit
must climb the tree.

I am no stranger to working hard.
I have done it all my life.

As a result I have become accustomed to expecting success in everything I do.

Some people call me lucky,
but I know better.

I do not know anyone
who has got to the top
without hard work.

That is the recipe.

It may not always
get you to the top,
but should get you
pretty near.

I do not wait for moods.

You accomplish nothing
if you do that.

Your mind must know
it has got to get down
to work.

I feel sorry for the person
who can't get
genuinely excited
about his work.

Not only will he
never be satisfied,
but he will never
achieve anything worthwhile.

W-22

I have always believed that
if you put in the work,
the results will come.

I don't do things half-heartedly.
Because I know if I do,
then I can expect
half-hearted results only.

I just feel that
I am in tune with
the right vibrations
of the universe
when I'm in the
process of working.

I learned
the value of hard work
by working hard.

If I am lonely — I work.

If I am worried or fearful — I work.

If I am discouraged or defeated — I work.

Work to me is the key to happiness.

If you cannot do great things,
do small things in great way.

If you do not want to work,
you have to work
to earn enough money

so that
you won't have to work.

W-28

If you neglect your work,
you will dislike it.

If you do it well,
you will enjoy it.

In order that a man may be happy,
it is necessary that he should
not only be capable of his work,
but a good judge of his work.

In order that people
be happy in their work,
three things are needed:

they must be fit for it;
they must not do too much of it;
and
they must have a sense of success in it.

It is easy
to make things look hard

but hard
to make things look easy.

W-32

It is not the hours
you put in your work
that counts,

it's the work you
put in the hours.

It is the quality of our work
which will please God
and not the quantity.

W-34

Laziness may appear attractive,
but work gives satisfaction.

Life is so simple
when you are
just doing your job.

W-36

Live neither in the past
nor in the future,
but let each day's work
absorb your entire energies,
and satisfy your widest ambition!

W-37

Loyal and efficient work
is a great cause.

Even though it may not be
immediately recognized,
ultimately it bears fruit.

Many people worry so much
about managing their careers,
but rarely spend
half that much energy
managing their lives.

I want to make my life
and not just my job,
the best it can be.

The rest will work itself out.

Men,
for the sake of getting a living
forget to live.

W-40

Men who do things
without being told
draw the most wages.

My grandfather once told me that
there were two kinds of people:

those who do the work and
those who take the credit.

He told me
to be in the first group;
there was much less competition.

My philosophy is that
not only are you
responsible for your life,
but doing the best at this moment
puts you in the best place
for the next moment.

No good work is ever done
while the heart is hot,
anxious and fretted.

W-44

Nobody can be successful
unless he loves his work.

W-45

Nobody can think straight
who does not work.

Idleness warps the mind.

Non-violence may not always work,
but violence never does.

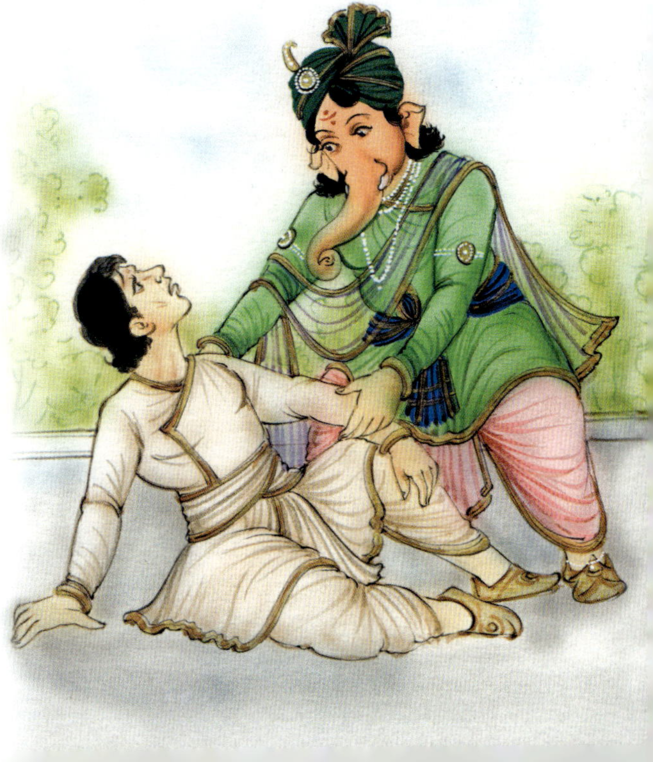

One kernel is felt in a hogshead;
one drop of water helps to swell the ocean;
a spark of fire helps to give light to the world.

None is too small, too feeble
and too poor to be of service.

Think of this and act.

W-48

Only work
which is the product of
inner compulsion
can have spiritual meaning.

Our chief defect is that we are more given to talking about things than to doing them.

W-50

Our great weariness comes
from work not done.

W-51

People are not the best
because they work hard;

they work hard
because they are the best.

People forget how fast you did a job;
but they remember
how well you did it.

W-53

People might not get
all they work for in this world,
but they must certainly
work for all they get.

Plans are only
good intentions unless
they immediately
degenerate into
hard work.

Pleasure in the job
puts perfection in the work.

Profit is a by-product of work;
happiness is its chief product.

W-57

Satisfaction lies more in the effort,
not in the attainment;

full effort is full victory.

Striving for success
without hard work
is like trying to harvest
where you haven't planted.

W-59

Success is peace of mind
which is a direct result of
self-satisfaction in knowing
that you did your best
to become the best
you are capable of becoming.

The best part of one's life is
the working part,
the creative part.

Believe me, I love to succeed.

However, the real spiritual and
emotional excitement is
in the doing.

The best preparation
for tomorrow is
to do today's work
superbly well.

The days you work
are the best days.

The harder I work,
the luckier I get.

W-64

The highest reward
for a person's toil
is not what he gets for it,
but what he becomes by it.

The highest reward
that God gives us
for good work
is the ability to do better.

The law of work seems unfair,
but nothing can change it;

the more enjoyment
you get out of your work,
the more money you will make.

W-67

The men and women
who got to the top were
those who did the jobs
they had in hand,
with everything they had —
energy, enthusiasm
and hard work.

The more I want to get
something done,
the less I call it work.

W-69

The only place
where success comes
before work
is in the dictionary.

The only thing
that overcomes
hard luck is
hard work.

The poor man with work
is happier than
the rich man in idleness.

The secret of joy in work
is contained in one word
— excellence.

To know
how to do something well
is to enjoy it.

W-73

The victory of success is half won when one gains the habit of work.

The world is full of willing people,
some willing to work,
the rest willing to let them.

There is joy in work.

There is no happiness
except in the realization
that we have
accomplished something.

There is nothing
better than that
a man should rejoice
in his own works,
for that is his heritage.

W-77

Think less about
what you want to do
and more about
what you are doing.

Until you find
that work
you enjoy,

enjoy that work
you find.

We forget that every good
that is worth possessing
must be paid for
in strokes of daily effort.

We postpone and postpone,
until those smiling possibilities
are dead.

W-80

What is earned with hard labour
is eaten with pleasure.

W-81

When a work lifts your spirits
and inspires bold
and noble thoughts in you,
don't look for any other
standard to judge by:
the work is good,
the product of a master craftsman.

When our eyes see our hands
doing the work of our hearts,
the circle of creation is complete inside us;

the doors of our souls fly open and
love steps forth to heal everything in sight.

When people go to work,
they should not leave
their hearts at home.

When work, commitment,
and pleasure
all become one
and you reach that deep well
where passion lives,
nothing is impossible.

W-85

When you cease
to make a contribution,
you begin to die.

W-86

When your work speaks for itself, don't interrupt.

Whenever there is
a hard job to be done
I assign it to a lazy man;

he is sure to find
an easy way of doing it.

W-88

Without rest, a man cannot work.

Without work, the rest does not give you any benefit.

Without work, all life goes rotten.

But when work is soulless,
life stifles and dies.

W-90

Work is love made visible.

And if you can't work with love
but only with distaste,
it is better that you
should leave your work
and sit at the gate of the temple
and take alms of those
who work with joy.

Work is not man's punishment.

It is his reward,
his strength and
his pleasure.

Work is the true luxury of life.

The busiest man is the happiest man.

Work is
the world's easiest escape
from boredom
and the only sure
fire road to success.

Work joyfully and peacefully,
knowing that right thoughts
and right efforts
will inevitably bring about
right results.

Work spares us from three evils:
boredom, vice, and need.

You can employ men and
hire hands to work for you,

but you must win their hearts
to have them work with you.

You do not become great
by trying to be great.

You become great
by wanting to do something,
and then doing it so hard
that you become great
in the process.

You know that it is only through work that you can achieve anything, either in college or in the life.

You make a living by
what you get,
but you make a life
by what you give.

W-100